THE BITCOIN AND BLOCKCHAIN BOOKLET

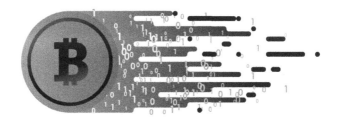

THE BEGINNER'S GUIDE TO GETTING STARTED WITH CRYPTOCURRENCY

The Bitcoin and Blockchain Booklet

Quick Read on How Crypto Works

ISBN: 978-1-950043-05-7

Publishing services provided by :  **Archangel Ink**

Where to Find the Best Cryptocurrency Content on the Web

Before you begin reading this book, I have a sweet deal to share with you. Best of all, it's totally free for you.

In addition to the information already provided in this book, be sure to subscribe to:

My YouTube channel for giveaways featuring $100 of Bitcoin Cash given to one listener for every new video: **https://www.youtube.com/cryptobeadles**

Twitter for the latest and greatest: **https://twitter.com/robertbeadles**

And my email list for the die-hard fans who want to get the biggest bang for their coin: **https://cryptobeadles.com/**

Follow me for in-depth content related to cryptocurrency and reach out with any questions. Enjoy and see you soon!

— Robert

TABLE OF CONTENTS

DISCLAIMER

Robert Beadles is the co-founder and creator of Monarch. Robert Beadles is not a professional financial adviser or financial expert. This is not financial advice. This is for education and entertainment purposes only. Always seek professional financial guidance before investing in anything. Investing is dangerous and you could lose all your money.

> "Cryptocurrency can be the greatest freedom or enslavement of the people, only time will tell which holds to be true."
>
> — *Robert Beadles AKA Crypto Beadles*

PREFACE

Bitcoin, crypto, and blockchain are hard for the masses to wrap their minds around. I'm reminded of a chat I had with my good friend and business partner UFC Legend Urijah Faber. He's a smart, hardworking guy and one of the best humans I know. In addition, he understands business, the world, the people in it and, obviously, the fight game. But as I started explaining to him how blockchain, security tokens, stable tokens, cryptocurrency, and Bitcoin works, he was getting more and more lost and said, "This is so complicated. It's no wonder people are getting hustled and scammed."

You know what? He's right! It is a whole new world of information and technology similar to when the car replaced the horse, the Wright brothers took flight, email took market share from the envelope, and when the internet came to be. It's very complicated and difficult for the average person to wrap their mind around, let alone use.

In this short booklet, I'm going to leave out much of the complexities and the exact science and try to break down this new world of blockchain, Bitcoin, and cryptocurrencies into something understandable.

My goal here is to get you familiar with how things fundamentally work, why they could change the world, and why everyone can benefit from using blockchain and crypto today.

People don't need to understand how and why the internet does what it does. They just want to be able to use it. I'll try to follow that recipe as we go along in this brief, digestible booklet.

Remember, this is not the be-all-and-end-all book. It's a booklet to open your mind and get you started. We don't cover everything here; we barely scratch the surface. This is your beginning, not the end.

I will provide resources where you can continue your education and give you places to start your crypto journey, if you so choose. If you're new to all this blockchain stuff, after reading this booklet you will have a far better grasp than most people in the world, who are still scratching their heads and asking, "What's blockchain?"

A quick mention too! You'll notice on the backside of each page it says "Notes." Use these pages to write down your thoughts, actions to take, etc.! Don't just read this booklet once and throw it down. Use this booklet to start your blockchain journey!

Now let's get going! Let's start with what we've all heard about, Bitcoin.

WHAT IS BITCOIN?

Think of a Bitcoin as a dollar and Satoshis as pennies

Bitcoin is basically digital money that anyone, anywhere, can use, without the need of banks or third parties. Its value and price is derived by supply and demand, just like anything else in this world. Bitcoin scares governments, banks, and big institutions, as they don't control it and, if people use Bitcoin over, say, the dollar, it could take power from these institutions.

Bitcoin was created by a person or group of people named Satoshi Nakamoto in 2008 and launched for the world to use in 2009. No one knows who Satoshi is. What we do suspect is that Bitcoin was created to combat or disrupt the global financial powers and networks we are all accustomed to using.

Notes

Bitcoin is a peer-to-peer digital currency that the user controls. The user can act as their own bank by holding this digital currency in an electronic wallet on their phone. The user can hold, spend, or receive Bitcoin anywhere in the world from their phone to pay for goods and services without the need of a bank or financial company. Banks or services that hold your money or give you access to it via our traditional financial system can freeze your money or take excessive fees for giving you access to it. This is not the case with Bitcoin and some other cryptocurrencies. You act as your own bank; you control your funds.

Think of it as sending credits to people from one smartphone app to another without anyone in between the sender and receiver.

Many people, however, don't spend Bitcoin. They simply hold on to it, as they think it will appreciate in price due to its scarcity.

Bitcoin *is* scarce. There will only be a total of 21 million Bitcoins ever and 5 to 6 million may have been lost forever. This means there is not enough Bitcoin for everyone. However, Bitcoins are made up of 100,000,000 Satoshis. Think of Satoshis as pennies and Bitcoins as dollars. Satoshis give people a way to spend their Bitcoin without having to spend an entire Bitcoin. And even though there are not enough Bitcoin to go around, there *are* enough Satoshis.

Notes

Bitcoin has gone from being worth pennies to twenty thousand dollars in value, then down to three thousand, then back up to ten thousand dollars. It's very volatile and the prices swing greatly due to many external factors. But it's also seen one of the highest returns on investment the world has ever seen in any asset class. Thus many simply hold on to it versus using it for goods and services.

All of the transactions used on the Bitcoin blockchain are transparent for the world to see and immutable, as no one can reverse or change these transactions. Bitcoin uses a decentralized blockchain to operate. This is where it gets confusing for many. What does centralized mean? What's decentralized? What is blockchain? And is decentralized really decentralized if people can change things? I'll discuss each of these topics in the most digestible format I can by using stories and leaving the science and intricacies out.

> "First, [Bitcoin] is the most secure transaction settlement layer in the world, so it's got to be worth something [...] it's the best performing asset class over the past ten years – it's outperformed S&P, DOW, NASDAQ, etc. during the longest bull run. It experienced two 85 percent drops during that time, but [it's] still up over 400 percent in the last two years."
>
> — *Anthony Pompliano*

Notes

WHAT IS BLOCKCHAIN?

Think of blockchain as being the network, and crypto being the "stuff" that's sent on or through the network

Here is a very easy way to visualize how the Bitcoin block-chain works in its most simple instance. This leaves out some of the complexities, but those aren't important to people trying to get a basic understanding.

Picture those old school rail carts with the open tops that workers would throw rock or coal in. Imagine it's on a railway, and the carts can only go forward. Can't visualize it? Think of the scene from *Indiana Jones and The Temple of Doom* where they are racing down the rails in one of those open-top carts with crazy people trying to kill them and overthrow their cart.

Notes

Each of these rail carts is a block, and there are miners on the side of the railway throwing confirmed transaction data from various users—what was transacted, who it was sent to, and when it was sent—in each of these carts. When one cart is full, a new cart is created and attached to the previous cart. The miners continue throwing the newest transaction data in that cart. Each miner is rushing to throw as much true user transaction data as possible in each of these carts, always trying to be the miner that throws the most true data into the carts. The carts are always going forward, never backward, and, once approved, the miners can't change what they had previously thrown in one of the blocks or carts.

Everyone in the world can see what's in these carts or blocks, as they are transparent with an open top. We can see what's what and who did what in each of the carts/blocks. The majority of miners agree to what's been thrown in each of these carts and agree to the rules of the railway and how the whole system works.

Sometimes, though, the miners disagree with each other on how much data they can throw in a cart/block or how fast they want the carts to go, so they fork the railway. They basically copy the existing cart and rail system and put it on a new track all of their own. Some miners stay with the old track, and some miners move over to the new track system. Sometimes the majority of miners have a problem with a current cart and rail system and decide to

Notes

upgrade it by making a copy of it, adding the upgrades and new features, and then putting it on a new railway.

These types of changes are called forks. A fork can occur anytime miners want something different or where they want to fix or upgrade the old system.

We see this time and time again. For example, with Bitcoin, some miners wanted bigger carts, so they forked the railway-blockchain and made Bitcoin Cash. Some miners stayed with the old cart system called Bitcoin while the other miners moved to a new rail system called Bitcoin Cash.

Bitcoin Cash added bigger carts so miners could add more data to each cart, making it faster and cheaper to get the carts and data out for the customers.

Remember that I said I would try to make this simple. I've left out things like validators and core programmers and haven't explained in great detail why these things happen. I've left out information on the huge computation power the miners use and the huge amounts of electricity it takes for the system to operate properly. For people who really want the nuts and bolts of how this works, look into what is called "Proof Of Work." This is the operating system, so to speak, that Bitcoin uses.

"As much as 73% of Chinese enterprises believe that blockchain is a top-five strategic priority, according to a

Notes

report by Big Four audit and consulting firm Deloitte released on June 27."

https://cointelegraph.com/news/deloitte-china-looking-to-use-blockchain-as-a-strategic-weapon

Notes

WHAT IS CRYPTOCURRENCY?

Think of cryptocurrency as different types of digital currency or credits

Cryptocurrency is basically a digital currency that uses cryptography (the conversion of data into a format that unauthorized users can't read) to help with its digital security. The word "crypto" comes from the underlying cryptography technology. Explaining this in detail would take a book unto itself. For further explanation on how cryptography is used in cryptocurrency, check out YouTube videos on the subject or read Andreas M. Antonopoulos's books *Mastering Bitcoin* and *The Internet of Money*.

Remember how we talked about the miners throwing data into the carts/blocks? Well, they are rewarded or "paid" in digital currency—cryptocurrency—for their work. Each

Notes

blockchain has its own cryptocurrency that usually only works on that one specific blockchain.

In addition to receiving the cryptocurrency for mining, people can buy these various cryptocurrencies from exchanges or companies like Monarch Wallet.

People do this because they feel the cryptocurrency will be worth more in the future or because they enjoy the freedom of using cryptos. The blockchain allows people to send cryptos to other people without the need of a bank, as I previously mentioned, and this appeals to a lot of people. Just like you can pass a dollar bill to your friend, you can pass a digital dollar to your friend's phone.

Sometimes these digital currencies become worthless, as people stop working on the blockchain or the public loses interest in the blockchain or crypto itself. But sometimes these cryptocurrencies become very valuable and the people holding them see a profit.

There are many use cases (situations a product or service could potentially be used for) for crypto outside of speculation.

Let's start with *stable tokens* or *stable coins.* These crypto currencies are typically backed by one dollar of real money or real assets. They're called stable cryptos because they are supposed to be worth one dollar. You see why this is useful? Imagine merchants who accept crypto trying to

Notes

maintain their budgets and profits when the price of traditional crypto could go up or down 80% in a day!

Using stable cryptos makes these price swings far less likely and allows the merchant the stability it requires to continue doing business. Next, imagine you are a Bitcoin holder, and you think the price is going to go up. Would you want to spend something like Bitcoin on a three-dollar cup of coffee? Would you spend Apple stock on coffee? What if Bitcoin ends up being worth 100 times what it's worth now? That could be a $300 cup of coffee. You know you'd be at least a little sad. Now imagine you used three dollars of stable tokens for the coffee. You could rest easy knowing that today, tomorrow, and the next day, it's still going to be worth close to three dollars.

There are also what are called *security tokens*, which people can "back" with a percentage of an asset like a stock, house, or artwork. Each token could be worth a percentage of the stock or house it represents. Think of these as digital tokens that have ownership in the underlying business or asset, much like a stock in traditional markets.

Utility tokens are tokens that are supposed to be used within a blockchain network to operate the system. They are designed like the Starbucks points you use to buy or get price breaks on Starbucks drinks. You wouldn't expect these to go up in value but many do, as Bitcoin itself has been classified as a utility coin and has seen over 400% gains this year alone.

Notes

Lastly, there are *privacy cryptos*, which work like utility cryptos but keep your transactions private so people can't see who you send your currency to.

Each currency typically only works on the blockchain it was created on. So Bitcoin, for instance, doesn't work on Ethereum and vice versa. Don't worry, I'll explain Ethereum a bit to ya as well. ☺

"Per the data collected from global statistics portals, the Bitcoin network posted $1.3 trillion worth of transactional volume in 2018. Within the same timeframe, PayPal recorded $578.65 billion worth of payment transactions. It was the second time in a row Bitcoin outran PayPal. In 2017, the digital currency network had posted 543.52 billion more transactional volume than the global firm."

https://www.newsbtc.com/2019/02/26/bitcoin-surpasses-paypal-in-yearly-transaction-volume-at-1-3-trillion/

Notes

WHAT IS ETHEREUM?

Think of Ethereum as Bitcoin
with contracts

Ethereum is the second most valuable and popular cryptocurrency after Bitcoin. It is designed like Bitcoin, but it allows you to add conditions and contracts.

For example, say I wanted to buy a car from you. You say it's awesome and that it runs and looks great, so I create a smart contract and send the money to it. I receive the car, and it's just as you said, so the smart contract sends you the money.

Let's now say it's a total bucket; it's not what I agreed to. The money from the smart contract would come back to me and the car would go back to you.

With Bitcoin, when you send money, there is no bringing it back. Once you send it, it's sent for good. If the car is a lemon, you're out of luck. Ethereum's smart contracts create rules that give you security and confidence in transactions that may have circumstances you want protection from.

Notes

For more information on how Ethereum works, check out my blog on CryptoBeadles.com.

Notes

WHAT DOES DECENTRALIZED MEAN?

Think of decentralized as meaning that no one person or company has total control

This is going to be super simplified, and I'm going to leave out all the complicated tech speak for you. I want you to get a basic understanding, not teach you how to create your own blockchain. I could do that, but it would take a far bigger booklet. ☺

Let's start off with how *decentralized* is defined by the Merriam-Webster dictionary:

Definition of decentralization

1
: the dispersion or distribution of functions and powers
// a *decentralization* of powers
specifically, government : the delegation of power from a central authority to regional and local authorities
// the *decentralization* of the state's public school system
// government *decentralization*

Notes

So in a nutshell, it means to take the authority, power, and rule from a central authority and give the power to the citizens. Instead of the king running the kingdom, the people run the kingdom.

Bitcoin uses this premise. It has thousands of people—miners—who are responsible for the security, reliability, and uptime of the network. It has over 99% uptime, too, with this structure.

These people all run the same software for the most part and all work independently, yet all follow the same pre-determined rules Satoshi Nakamoto wrote into the initial code. If these miners don't play fair or try to game the system, they are kicked out of the club.

Imagine a group of people who all belong to a club that was started by one person, who wrote a manual on what is expected of each member. Let's say to enter the club you have to know a predefined handshake. It has to be done perfectly or you can't get in.

If you pass the handshake test, you have to do a defined set of tasks, and everyone has to do them identically, individually, perfectly, or they too will be kicked out of the club.

If you do the handshake and complete your tasks perfectly, you will be compensated from the income the club generates from the completed tasks. Any variance of the

Notes

handshake or tasks from the original manual, and that member isn't paid and gets kicked out.

This is a super loose example of how Bitcoin works. You have thousands of people who don't have to know each other but have to run the same software on their computers and do everything as the manual says. If they do, they will be rewarded in Bitcoin for keeping the Bitcoin network up and running. Anyone can join, but you must follow the rules.

Some people have created "pools," where groups of people work together to maintain the network and, through strength in numbers, are rewarded more than just a single person running one computer. Many hands make light work, so to speak.

This is super simplified but I hope you understand that there are many computers all running the same code to keep the Bitcoin network alive. They can work together or work independently, but they all have to follow the rules.

Notes

WHAT DOES CENTRALIZED MEAN?

Think of centralized as meaning that one company or person has total control

Centralized is basically the opposite of decentralized. The king runs the kingdom. Think about a bank. They don't want a ton of people looking at their books or having access to their system, so they typically have an internal team who is responsible for keeping their network up and running, and they don't allow outsiders in to see what's what or to benefit from their network.

This can be hazardous, as we know power corrupts and absolute power corrupts absolutely. But it does have some advantages. If there is a problem, one person or one company can be held accountable. A centralized system can also offer far greater customer support. Let's take a look at the positives and negatives.

Notes

WHAT ARE SOME OF THE PROS AND CONS OF DECENTRALIZED AND CENTRALIZED NETWORKS?

In theory, a truly decentralized network would be a living, breathing network without any one person or organization controlling it. It would be free of the confines of a ruling entity. It would survive as long as people kept running the code and supporting the network.

However, many decentralized networks are not really decentralized, as someone or some company may have created an unfair advantage when the blockchain was first created or left back doors for the creators to later change things.

For instance, if the creator owns a large percentage of the cryptocurrency used on that blockchain, they may be incentivized to do things contrary to what the public would want to gain more profits or advantages for themselves. We have seen this many times in cryptocurrency. They do this through shady practices such as pump-and-dump schemes.

Notes

A pump-and-dump is when someone puts a large amount of one specific cryptocurrency on an exchange, making it look like there is a high demand for this crypto. This causes the price to shoot up, and more and more people buy the crypto. When the value hits whatever target price the initial person or group had as a goal, they sell all that crypto, which dumps the price drastically. Anyone not part of that group can lose a ton of money, as the price will most likely drop below what they paid for it. These schemes are highly immoral and have devastated good people.

Let's get back on track now and talk about decentralized versus centralized. Let's look at Bitcoin and Amazon as examples here. Bitcoin is decentralized. If you send money to the wrong person or lose your private seed (I'll explain later what a seed is), you've totally lost your Bitcoin. If you need help navigating the use of Bitcoin, there's no customer service department; you may have to ask the community or other users how to solve your problem. These people may have a shady agenda and try to scam you out of your Bitcoin.

With Amazon, there is customer service. If you buy something you don't like, you can send it back and get your money back. If you lose access to your account, they can restore it for you. Their customer service is there to help you and typically has your best interest in mind.

However, if you're a merchant, Amazon will always put the customer above you, right or wrong. They can freeze your funds. They may try to take your business right out

Notes

from under you, if it's profitable enough, then call it by a different name.

With Bitcoin, you are in total control of everything but it comes with a price. You must be aware you are acting as your own bank and acting as your own monarch, so to speak, so you have no one to turn to but yourself if things go bad.

I believe there needs to be a compromise, a hybrid. The important data you want to own and keep must stay in your control and should be decentralized. The part of your data for which you want ease of use and speed should be centralized.

To date, no one has done this well. When someone or some company does, I believe we will all win. My company Monarch has made that our mission. We need customer service we can count on, but we also need total ownership of our funds and data so no one but us can access or share it.

I don't want to go on a rant here, but the issues in our current centralized system are obvious if you look at just a few of the major corporations and credit bureaus that have been hacked or have leaked or sold our data. The hybrid centralized/decentralized system I'm thinking of would make this impossible. In my system, we are in control of our sensitive data, and the only potential for harm would come from ourselves, not a third party or centralized company. Also, in a decentralized service, a person

Notes

would have to hack thousands of computers to access our data, while a smart hacker could access all our data in one hack to a centralized server.

Decentralized services offer a plethora of benefits and a handful of weaknesses. A hybrid solution, I believe, would solve these issues.

Notes

WHAT IS A PRIVATE SEED, KEYS?

Think of your private key as the pin code to your ATM card. Think of your private seed as an exact map to your buried treasure.

Here again, I'm going to keep this as simple as possible.

With a centralized system, you are relying on other people or companies to keep your funds safe. If they go out of business or steal your funds, you're screwed.

There is a saying in crypto, "Not Your Keys, Not Your Crypto." This simply means that if someone is holding on to your money, it may not be your money. They could lose it, steal it, whatever it. With crypto, you can download wallets that are decentralized, like the one my company, Monarch Wallet offers. Meaning no one has

Notes

king-like control over your info or funds. You can be in total control and be the monarch of your funds and info.

When you download a decentralized wallet like the Monarch Wallet, it will give you twelve words, your private "seed," that you must write down and keep safe. If you ever lose your phone or delete the wallet, you can re-download a Monarch Wallet on a new phone, and your money will come back to you like magic when you simply type those twelve words back into it.

However, if you share those twelve words with someone, intentionally or accidentally, they could steal all your money. And if you lose those twelve words, you could lose all your money. It's a scary but empowering thing. You are in total control of your entire kingdom of funds. No one else.

As they say in Spiderman, with great power comes great responsibility.

Never lose or share your seed or keys. If you do, you lose your crypto.

Notes

WHAT ABOUT OTHER CRYPTOCURRENCIES?

Think of other cryptocurrencies as being like monies from different governments. Each government has their own dollar

Most cryptocurrencies are a copy or clone of Bitcoin or Ethereum. A person made changes to them maybe to allow a specific industry the ability to use their blockchain or maybe just to scam people out of money.

There are tons of use cases for blockchain and crypto, but most do it solely to raise money for themselves and their team, not to add value to the world.

It's much like the internet bubble. Many businesses were created, but only a handful survived and succeeded. Today, anyone can create their own blockchain or crypto-currency with just a few clicks of their mouse, and not all are created equal. Some people bring real value to block-chain that will change the world, make no mistake about it, but many will fail.

Notes

China and other countries, and some central banks and financial institutions, are rumored to be launching their very own cryptocurrencies that they will introduce their citizens and users to. This will speed up adoption of cryptocurrency, but it will be super centralized, and we will have to wait and see if it's for good or evil.

Even Facebook is launching their own cryptocurrency called Libra and there are two to three billion people and over 80 million businesses using Facebook!

These cases alone will be massive for awareness and entry to cryptocurrency. When the masses start using government or Facebook crypto, it may open their eyes to all the other cryptos out there like Bitcoin and all the value and freedom those cryptos offer.

Notes

WHAT IS AN ICO?

Think of an ICO as a Kickstarter campaign, but typically you don't get equity in the company

In 2017 there was a huge surge of ICOs—initial coin offerings—which is the cryptocurrency version of an IPO, an initial public offering. Companies use ICOs to raise money, and investors receive a new cryptocurrency token in exchange, hoping it will provide a good return on investment. Many people used the Ethereum blockchain to create a token for themselves to try and raise a bunch of money for their ideas. Many of these ICOs were scams or just couldn't deliver on their promises.

Security token offerings (STOs) are basically the same thing but for security tokens. These are supposed to be backed by a security like real estate or future profits in a company. They are typically for accredited investors or people not in the United States.

Then we have IEOs—initial exchange offerings—which are basically an ICO done on a cryptocurrency exchange, where the exchange supposedly vetted the company and

Notes

made it safer for the public. This is also dangerous as many exchanges just prey on their users and could be a part of the scam.

All of these are dangerous and require a ton of expertise, guidance, and disposable money to play with. Ninety-nine percent of these will lose your money, in my opinion.

Hundreds of billions of dollars were raised, gained, and lost with these methods of raising capital. I don't want to spend a lot of time explaining these in further detail, as these are so dangerous this is more of a hazard warning than education. Only 1% might...might...possibly succeed.

I don't want you gambling on these. And make no mistake, it is gambling. People have used ICOs like Kickstarter to fund their ideas. Anyone can do it. Heck, you just read this, and you could go do it, but that doesn't mean it will work. It's only as good as the idea, person, team, tech, marketing, and support behind it.

Many will fail and cost the investors a ton of money. A handful will win and make their investors and team very wealthy. That's why it still exists, like any blackjack table.

FUNDS RAISED IN 2017

Total raised: **$6,226,689,449**
Number of ICOs: **875**
https://www.icodata.io/stats/2017

Notes

WHERE TO BUY

The cryptocurrencies I feel are safest for me to buy are Bitcoin, Bitcoin Cash, and Ethereum. (This is not financial advice and I am not a financial adviser.) There are many points of sale, such as the countless exchanges and local Bitcoin dot coms, but all of those cryptos are available to purchase directly from your bank account or credit card via the Monarch Wallet. I feel this is the safest way to buy cryptocurrency because you use our centralized solution to purchase the crypto but your funds are stored decentralized so only the user-purchaser has control of them.

Notes

WHY BUY?

Typically people buy cryptocurrencies for speculation. They feel the price they paid for it is less than what it one day will be worth.

Others hold it as currency that they simply feel is more stable than government-controlled fiat currencies or, again, they feel it will be worth more in the future than their government's currency.

Then there are people who simply don't trust their government's monetary policies. They see inflation and hyperinflation erode their currency, like in Venezuela. People there could make $100 a day in wages and it could be worth less than $5 by day's end.

By using things like stable tokens or possibly Bitcoin, they have a good idea of what their wages will remain at. In addition, people can take these cryptocurrencies and spend them anywhere in the world without having to worry about third parties or conversion fees from one fiat currency to another. For example, if you are paid in pesos but want US dollars, you would have to pay a conversion fee to someone to convert it. With things like stable

Notes

tokens, the volatility and price swings are mostly removed and there are few to no conversion fees.

Then too there is a movement to take the printing power away from the government and central banks and restore it to the people. Using the right cryptocurrencies, this is, in theory, partially achievable.

Notes

HOW TO SAFELY STORE CRYPTO

There are numerous ways to store your crypto. There are exchanges where you can simply leave your funds. You can buy a hardware wallet and store currencies there. You can print a paper wallet. Or you can simply download an app.

I am going to recommend to you what I do, what's easiest and I feel safest.

I obviously will show bias here as the builder, co-founder, and president of the Monarch Wallet, but I trust it and that's why I will share my way of doing things here with you.

For everyday use of crypto in commerce, simply download the Monarch Wallet and buy or send whatever supported tokens or coins to it. Easy peasy. Just know that if someone puts a gun or pipe wrench to your head, you'll probably give them the crypto on your phone. Think of this method as being like your leather wallet. How much cash would you flash or keep on you? Treat this the same way.

Notes

For long-term safe holding of crypto you don't plan on using soon—think of this as your retirement or savings account—I recommend the following:

Simply grab an old smartphone you don't use any longer or go on eBay and buy an old Android or Apple phone. Download the Monarch Wallet app to this phone and transfer all the coins and tokens that Monarch supports to the app. For any currencies Monarch doesn't support, simply download that currency's decentralized wallet to the phone as well.

Once all your currencies are in the wallet or wallets, simply remove the SIM card, turn off the Wi-Fi, put the phone in airplane mode, and store it somewhere safe and accessible to you. This way no hacker or thug can gain access to your funds.

When you want to send your funds somewhere, simply get the phone, turn on the Wi-Fi, send your funds, and then put it back in airplane mode with the Wi-Fi off. This simple method is far more secure than paying big money for hardware wallets that have constant updates and may have bugs that need to be fixed before usage. And it's safer than using paper wallets, which can disappear in a single washing-machine accident, or using an exchange that could steal your funds or simply go out of business.

Notes

USE CASES

As we've mentioned, Bitcoin is peer-to-peer digital currency. Now anywhere in the world you go, you and only you have control of your money. If stored properly.

We've all tried to use our ATM or credit card only to find out the bank or credit card company won't let us. We've had liens or had the IRS take money right out of our bank accounts. We've had credit card processors take money from our accounts and pay the customer back. We've had garnishments put on our bank accounts. We've seen governments print currencies into extinction. And we've seen the value of our currencies drop due to inflation. There are a thousand other examples.

None of this is an issue with a truly decentralized crypto-currency or wallet.

We finally have total control of our money.

In addition to using it as currency or a store of value, there are countless use cases for blockchain in general.

Because decentralized or public blockchains are transparent, we can see the transactions, or data, stored on them. Now imagine if we used this for food, medications, or

Notes

logistics. We could see where it came from, how old it is, where it is, or how much there is.

It could also be helpful for real-estate transactions or purchases, making ownership known and absolute, cutting down on countless boxes of physical paper for each asset.

Companies could create their own tokens that their customers could use like digital coupons, gift cards, or price break mechanisms.

Using smart contracts, we could drastically eliminate the need for attorneys because we'll all know exactly who gets what and when without the need for intermediaries and the countless paper documents that attorneys love to charge us for drafting.

Merchants can use things like MonarchPay and no longer have to worry about chargebacks or high transaction fees. Merchants can use it today for one-time transactions or recurring transactions, and it could cost them less than 1% in total fees, where credit cards, PayPal, and Patreon can cost up to 12% per transaction and freeze your funds!

Some say our cars will drive and navigate us around the globe using blockchain, and we'll explore the galaxy using it as well! These are just a few of the multitudes of examples there are for how to use this incredible technology called blockchain. In addition, I believe every physical asset like stocks, bonds, securities, and real estate will

Notes

have a cryptocurrency counterpart for easy sending and receiving and for proof of ownership.

Much remains to be seen, but peer-to-peer digital money that we the people have total control of is a pretty incredible start!

Notes

WHAT IS THE MONARCH WALLET?

Think of Monarch as an app that makes you the monarch of all your finances and blockchain services

As mentioned, I am the builder, co-founder, and president of the Monarch Wallet and by now you may want to know what it is and what it does. So here is a brief summary:

Monarch Wallet is free to download and allows people to buy and sell some of the most popular cryptocurrencies. It allows people to send, store, and receive cryptocurrencies. Qualified people can also earn up to 8% interest a year on certain cryptocurrencies. It has a built-in decentralized exchange so people can trade tokens. It has a built-in portfolio tracker so users can track their holdings, gains, and losses, and a news aggregator so the user can keep up on all their favorite cryptocurrency news. And it is decen-

Notes

tralized so only the user has access to their funds, seed, and keys.

In the near future, it will give the user access to the best services and companies in crypto and blockchain that we partner with through a one-login experience.

Users will no longer need to download countless apps. They would just have the Monarch Wallet app and have one login for all our partners through it.

We have done this already with four incredible cryptocurrency companies.

It's incredible what we have built, if I may say so myself, and we hope to see you here!

Notes

WHAT IS MONARCHPAY?

Think of MonarchPay as an additional way to receive funds from your users with no chargebacks and super low fees

MonarchPay is a decentralized platform created by me and Monarch's other co-founder, that allows anyone, including merchants, to accept payments in stable or unstable cryptocurrency for goods or services.

It has many of the features you would expect from a centralized solution but uses smart contracts to ensure payments go directly from the user to the merchant or vice versa, with no one in between. It can cost less than 1% of the transaction price.

Credit cards, PayPal, and other payment methods can cost merchants above 4%. Patreon is higher yet at 10%

Notes

and rumored to soon be up to 12% per transaction. With all of those drawbacks, the merchant can also suffer things called chargebacks.

Let's say you're a merchant and you sell Bob a shirt. He uses his credit card, receives the shirt, then calls his credit card company and says he never received it. The credit card company charges you back, takes Bob's money from you, and gives it back to Bob. Bob keeps the shirt. Not cool, right? This happens every day, but never with MonarchPay.

MonarchPay can be used for one-time purchases or recurring daily, weekly, or monthly subscription-type charges and allows the merchant access to the user's basic data so they can run their business just like they would any other payment system.

This doesn't have to replace the merchant's other payment methods; this can be an add-on. Think of it as another tool—pay with credit card, pay with Venmo, pay with PayPal, or pay with MonarchPay.

The best part is, it's available NOW at MonarchPay.com The fee for using it is around 1% of the transaction value and soon, using Monarch Tokens, it could be as low as .5% per transaction!

It's currently available on desktop and soon it will be available within the Monarch Wallet on mobile as well. Crypto can change the world, peeps!

Notes

CLOSING THOUGHTS

A case for crypto

Remember earlier when I mentioned the early days of the internet and email, how people had a hard time wrapping their heads around it, and how people thought the Wright brothers were nuts for trying to take to the sky? Well, we are very much in that stage for cryptocurrency and blockchain.

Can you imagine a world with no internet now? No social media, no online businesses, no streaming movies, no virtual meetings!

Imagine having to take a horse or a car across the US from LA to NY or take a boat from the US to Asia instead of a passenger jet? Imagine having to hand address an envelope, lick a stamp, and wait days, weeks, or months for a reply instead of sending an email where we can convey our message and get a response globally in seconds.

Our society would implode overnight without these things we take for granted daily.

Notes

This is where I believe we are headed for blockchain and cryptocurrency. Imagine having the ability to safely send, store, and receive your money, anywhere, anytime in the world with no one to squeeze fees from you, freeze your funds, or outright take them from you!

Think about a currency with a value that is stable or increasing every year versus decreasing due to the excessive printing of money by our governments and central banks and inflation eroding our dollar's value, year after year.

Imagine a world where you could send digital proof of ownership of your house or stock or other asset instead of trying to find the paperwork or deeds from decades or centuries past.

Imagine instantly being able to know where your food, merchandise, or medication came from and went, what's in it, who made it, and how much is left with a simple scan or click of a button.

Imagine a world with 95% fewer lawyers. ☺ Smart contracts could drastically cut the need for attorneys to enforce contracts or seek remedies for people and companies failing to comply with contracts.

These are just a couple of the thousands of examples I could give you for why companies like Walmart, Alibaba, HP, ICE, the People's Bank of China, Bank of America, Mastercard, VISA, American Express, IBM, Dell, Intel, Sony, Amazon, eBay, Fidelity, JP Morgan, CME, CBOE, Circle,

Notes

Facebook, the Fed, and countless other monster corporations have either entered cryptocurrency and blockchain or soon will.

These are some of the largest, most profitable, smartest companies, banks, and governments in the world who are going to be using and selling their blockchain services to the world, whether we want them or not.

A few fun facts:

69% of banks are experimenting with permission-based blockchains - Tech In Asia, 2017

Blockchain technology could save banks between $8-12 billion annually - Silicon, 2017

50% of banks are working with a fintech startup to augment their blockchain capabilities - Tech in Asia, 2017

The question you have to ask yourself is, will you be one of the ones saying that flight isn't possible, email won't replace regular mail, or the internet doesn't have any uses for today? Or will you be the person traveling the world, streaming their favorite shows on Netflix, profitably

Notes

running their business, and keeping in touch with people everywhere at any time using the internet?

Blockchain and crypto have a long way to go before they are simple for people to use, and that's currently the biggest hurdle it has today for mass adoption. It's still too complicated for the average person to wrap their minds around it, let alone use it. That's why we built the Monarch Wallet. It's the one downloadable app that allows you to safely buy, sell, send, store, receive, and track various cryptocurrencies. And soon it will allow access to all the best services and blockchain businesses.

A one-stop shop, so to speak, a one-login solution. One app versus the forty apps you would need to access all these companies or their services. The Monarch Wallet allows its users to access these super valuable resources and tools through one account, one login, and one app.

This process will get simpler and simpler to use, too, and people will be able to use cryptocurrency and blockchain without having to know how it works. Simply like using Facebook—you click that little thumbs-up button and you like something. You don't have to be a master programmer to figure it out.

That's our goal, what we have been building and what's free for the world to download, today.

Notes

Monarch empowers the user. It allows them to be the monarch, the king or queen of their digital and financial lives, from the palm of their hand.

It's things like Monarch that will bring the masses in, not what we currently have in blockchain. It will take time, but it is my belief and the belief of millions of others that blockchain and crypto is coming and we can all benefit from it.

With that said, I have to issue a warning. I've often said crypto can either enslave or empower the people. If a government mandates their own sanctioned cryptocurrency and then forces social engineering, this would allow them to track every person and transaction, and freeze, confiscate, or disavow certain funds from the system. In contrast, things like Bitcoin are great for the world as it empowers people, giving them all of the power over their assets. But we have to choose wisely what cryptocurrency or blockchain we use. Most use it for speculation currently, but soon we'll be using it for our gas, groceries, travel, retirement accounts, proving asset ownership, running our businesses—you name it! The sky's the limit!

In my opinion, we are living in the greatest moment in human history and what comes from blockchain and cryptocurrency breakthroughs and adoption will absolutely change the world and I'm not alone in thinking this way:

Notes

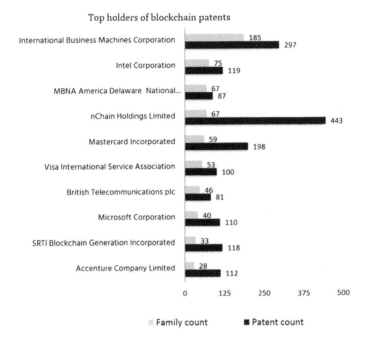

Top holders of blockchain patents

Sourced From https://www.lexology.com–June 12, 2019.

Notes

A BIT ABOUT BEADLES

CRYPTO **BEADLES**

I'm a Christian, husband, father, business builder, inventor, educator, and investor.

I met my wife, Nicole, when I was 14, and we have been together ever since. We married and had our first child, Aaron, at 17. Our second son, Kyle, came along when we were 21. Nicole is my best friend and partner.

Through the grace of God and hard work, we went from being on government aid, welfare, and food stamps to survive to our companies making millions of dollars per month. We're one of the largest employers in California's Central Valley.

I educate people in blockchain via my TV Show on BizTV called *Crypto Beadles*. My son and I have a channel on YouTube called Crypto Beadles where we bring on the founders of blockchain projects so viewers can learn about the founders and projects. We give away $100 of

Notes

cryptocurrency on every video, every Monday, live on the air at 1 PM PST, to help others get in blockchain.

In addition, I write articles posted to our website CryptoBeadles.com to help educate, and I speak freely on Twitter as @RobertBeadles as well.

We travel the globe speaking at conferences to further blockchain education and adoption. I read the Bible daily, am constantly learning about countless subjects, have created one of the largest construction service companies in California, am an avid real-estate investor and author, have patented numerous devices and applications, am the CEO of Splash Factory Blockchain Development House and co-founder and builder of the Monarch Wallet, and I genuinely try to make Earth a better place for every-one while I'm here.

Notes

WHO IS MONARCH?

Robert Beadles – President-Co-founder
Sneh Bhatt – CEO-Co-Founder

An incredible team of over 30 amazing developers and social media professionals

Advisers:

Eric Ly – Co-Founder of LinkedIn
Roger Ver – Founder of Bitcoin.com
David Zimbeck – Creator of the smart contract
Gee Hwan Chuang – Founder of Listia
Dmitri Nazarov – Founder of Genesis Vision
Nimrod May – Ex-Head Of Disney Marketing
Damon Nam – Founder of Coin
And many more

Visit www.MonarchWallet.com for more info

Notes

RESOURCES AND TOOLS

CryptoBeadles.com/Blog
Crypto Beadles YouTube Channel
@RobertBeadles on Twitter
MonarchWallet.com
MonarchPay.com
TradingView Sessions
BizTV
AmazingCrypto.com

Contact:

CryptoBeadles@gmail.com

Thank You for Reading

Want to know more?

Don't forget to follow me on social media for the most up-to-date content in the cryptocurrency world. I've done my best to include the most relevant and up-to-date information in this book, but things change quickly! Follow me here to stay informed:

> Subscribe to my YouTube channel for giveaways featuring $100 of cryptocurrency given to one listener for every new video: https://www.youtube.com/cryptobeadles

> Follow me on Twitter for the latest and greatest on crypto: https://twitter.com/robertbeadles

> And for the die-hard fans, you can join my email list to get the biggest bang for your coin: https://cryptobeadles.com/

Please do not hesitate to connect with me if you have any questions about this book, or if you would like to discuss your BITCOIN and BLOCKCHAIN endeavors.

I enjoy connecting with readers and would be happy to hear from you!

— Robert

A Quick Favor Please?

A quick favor before you go.

Would you please leave a quick review for this book?

Reviews are very important and help authors like me to share our experience and services so we can help more people and influence better financial structures for tomorrow.

Please take a quick minute to leave this book an honest review. I promise it doesn't take long, but it can help me reach more readers just like you.

Thank you so much reading.

— *Robert*

Made in the USA
Las Vegas, NV
11 December 2020

12407935R00066